Dedicate to

Cindy Rohrich (R.I.P.)

-forever lost, love-

FOR FURTHER ENQUIRES CONTACT
NATHANIEL JARROD- PH. 0458735522

ISBN:978-1-4709-1515-5

Table of Contents

- Footsteps in fire....Edaff Pard
- Lay....Dee Watts
- Life forever....Delroy Greene
- Promises of below....Joanne Axl
- Sleeping death....Prindle Rand
- Lingering....Keilor Cheswick
- Of death....Aaron Ungle
- Master of death and disaster....Anonymous
- Moving darkness....Richard Feldar
- Murky waters....Randle Westfolk
- Soothed soul, the....Alton Edwards
- Merciful death....Rakkis Redheart
- My ghostly friend....Ann Daist
- My master's slave....Jar Warwick
- My second coming....Arid Arbrotten
- Be no more....Estrel Olive
- All about death....Terry Powell
- Killer....Ish Baglisch
- Free from Hell....Malcolm Fiddler
- Better you than me....Harriot Mare
- Buried....Gypsy White
- Burning game....Schipp Thane
- Decade of decay....Angel Appenstock

- Black enough....Glen Glielg
- Caressing dark, the....Elios Jones
- God's immortality, the....Swit Reason
- Bliss of death....Farra Kinkle
- Nameless....Virginia Vallens
- To set free a soul....Glen Glielg
- Homeless....Ann Daist
- Nevermore....Peise Woolworm
- Night forever....Anglish Dippea
- No path is clear....Aaron Ungle
- In black....Joanne Axl
- Soul, the....Dane Storm
- In black you choke....Orran Ericson
- Releasing Reaper....Delroy Greene
- Soul in death assisted, the....Keilor Cheswick
- In death....Crane Imbrose
- A final self-kill....Glen Glielg
- Souls in the shadows....Alse Olden
- In rotten grave....Gypsy White
- A soul in darkness....Verone Dorn
- Spirit choir, the....Agnus Adgit
- Dying, the....David fistripper
- Grave sleep....AaronUngle
- Spirits....Richard Feldar

SPECTERS

By Rakkis Redheart

Specters haunt my every move
Put me in a blackened mood
Twist my mind until I despise
My own face I must disguise

Specters haunt me
Doom I do see
Death courts my every move
It will release this blackened mood

Specters gather overhead
Tell me soon I will be dead
Then be theirs to devour
This is the hour

Specters invade my every pour
I scratch my skin until it is raw
I scream a prayer to God, above
For me there is no love

Specters take my soul away
To a dark room where it stays
They eat me
They beat me
They scream and they teach me
The meaning of pain

BONES

By Estrel Olive

I depart the world without flare
Open your eyes, I will be there
A single tear will spill to the sand
Water is precious in this barren land

The midday sun my soul encapture
I die and be dead without the rapture
As decay surely, slowly enters
I know I've failed recent ventures

I turn my face to my body, laying
still
As skin sears, melts and peals
Then altogether falls completely
From bones that are connected neatly

The bits that stick to the bone
No longer mine, vultures own
Those bones that are shining bright
In gleaming sun they're turning
white

LISTLESS

By Aaron Ungle

Longing for life
Insidious Strife
Shocking state
Thickening fate
Love be lost
Endlessly
Sibilant souls
Speak silently

VIRTUALITY

By Aaron Ungle

Living on the virtuality
Taking leave of reality
Kill all and leave none
Call it work, not fun

Diving off the deep end
Driving fast around that bend
No thoughts on what's coming
Got to keep on running

No tomorrow, today's here
Yesterday's over, shedding a tear
Fighting to breathe
Wishing to leave
Having no needs but doing the deed

Tomorrow's here
Shedding a tear
Yesterday is buried amongst the
monsters of the past

All those monsters, black and mean
Worse at night than in daytime seen
They hunt you down, a measly bite
Give you such and awful fright

They tell you now, “Remember this
Your weak flesh my teeth will kiss
Have no Gods
Have only me
Because my evil does become thee”

LONE SOUL

By Ish Baglisch

It becomes me
What I've done
And I know
The darkness won

Eyes are full
Of golden tears
And from out
A lone soul peers

A desperate plea
In silent scream
An awful, waking
Madman's dream

It will end
And I know
To Heaven's light
This soul won't go

THE WAY OF THE AFTERLIFE

By Ish Baglisch

Reflect the days
Passed into past
All washed away
Hoping they will last

Drift under the moon
In the wind's slight sigh
Perhaps it's too soon
To understand why

Become the air
So light and flighty
Tickle the bear
So great and mighty

In the lungs of great beast
Feel tremors of power
Upon you he feasts
No need to cower
Harm you not
Does mighty creature
Air not rot
This be my feature

Drifting sunward looking down
Bear, he plays upon the ground
Floating earthbound looking up
Heaven is the wine in eternity's cup

Roaming soul lost to all
Knows naught of an Angel's fall
Sees about him many auras
Some do float, others are soarers

If needs be oceans in which to float
Souls require one
If earth be the castle, Heaven the
moat
With castles souls are done
Be it of sand which oceans wipe
clean
Under mighty sun
The ocean remains and within souls
beam
And all have one

So death come swiftly
Death come sweet
Release this soul
From fettering meat

Let it drift
Let it fly
Let it consul
When loved ones cry

Let it touch
Both light and strong
Let it judge
And right the wrongs

Be it bright
This aura, mine
I have no body
But aura shine

When dream the young
Of better things
Hold not them back
For a miracle it brings

Guiding hands are the winds soft blow
Within it flies the black-eyed crow
Side by side with souls so bright
To fly in wind is pure delight
Come my friend, enjoy the years
Come my friend, shed no tears
For if you could you're only beginning
A journey worthy of Angel's singing

Follow the path which chosen you
See the end, may your tread be true
Because at the end your colors show
We souls are but colors as one day
you'll know

Bear me down
Hold me in
This is but
The beginning

Breathe me in
Sigh me out
Trust the one
Whose name I shout

He be next
Upon the list
Which Angels keep
Which all souls kissed

The lists of dead
Belong to us
My name is there
A name to trust

I have an aura
Mostly green
Some have said
Red they've seen
A corona of blue
Brilliant and iridescent
And in my middle
A silver crescent

A silver eighth moon
As have we all
A heart of energy
That does call
The blue, the green, the red of my soul
To writhe and crawl
And be me
A multicolored shawl

A multicolored shawl
To be worn lightly
To be draped
When sun shines brightly
The less we love
The less we wear
So have a care
And beware

If you wish to shine brightly
Throughout life tread lightly
Treat others with respect
And in turn expect
They treat you well
Your fears dispel

Now, in the present
Breathe my soul
I'm with the wind
Exhale me whole

LOST REDEMPTION

By Glen Glielg

Death comes calling
As nighttimes falling
Stealing souls and taking lives
Only vigilance survives

A soul once white has now the black
On this soul God turned his back

Damned redemption's lost
Understand, your life's the cost

Live through this and you might see
Your soul will never be free
The fires seer your soul away
Die you do without delay

Damned, redemption's lost
Understand, your life's the cost

Of all the possible roads to be
trodden
You walk alone, a corpse rotten
Of all the hearts which cease to beat
The dying doves lay at your feet

Damnation, redemption's sought
Incarceration, coffin caught

No parting breath to be released
Can bring about a corpse deceased
Can obtain the truth of God
A holy scepter or glowing rod

The Gods do not care for swine,
below
They let you rot; eaten, beaten slow
All this pain you now are feeling
Makes you wish for an altar of
healing

WELCOMED DEATH

By Arid Arbrotten

Bloody tears I cry
I wish to die
The door has shut
A wound you've opened up

My life is fallen
As I am, too
My heart is pierced
Pierced by you

Eternal agony descends
My heart never mends
Your claws tear
Your claws rend

Death, you are welcome
I have opened the door
Death, sweet Death
I live no more

UNTETHERED

By Alex Edwards

Disaster takes you to the grave
Say goodbye, no soul to save
Since the end did finally come
To Eternity your soul did run

Many men a legacy left
A memory bereft that final breath
What amounts to a life?
Whom would want to live life twice?

The death of many has caused relief
The numbers which haunt, beyond belief
Brief the life taken from us
With a prayer to Heaven trust

Opened a wound in your soul
As body left from blessed hole
Briefly surveying all whom have gathered
Then to float and live untethered

WHEN I DIE

By Aaron Ungle

Swim little fish
Swim with all your might
Shark is right behind you
He knows how to fight

Death comes to all
In his own sweet time
He will come to me
Without rhythm or rhyme

What will I say to Reaper, grim?
What will I be thinking when vision grows dim?
Where will I be after this event?
In Heaven with my God or to the Devil sent?

Today there is no worry
Reaper worries me not
I believe that when I die
In my coffin rot

LIFE'S A FAZE

By Ish Baglisch

The time will come and I will follow
All the paths which lead to sorrow
In a word, I come for you
Damned you'll be when I am through

The eternal plight of mortal man
To face a judgement or be damned
The symptom is worse than the cure
Is your heart pure?

It's doubtless you've been the one
whom has been sinning
Ends occur so there can be
beginnings

If forever you walk an endless maze
Remember, life is just a faze

WHERE GOES THE SOUL?

By Jamess Johns

Where goes the soul long after
breathing?
Where goes the soul?
The soul we are needing

Virtuous sound of chimes
The wind does settle
Hear the sound of a dropping petal

Where goes the soul whom does guide
us?
Where goes the soul whom does give
trust?
Soul, don't forego guidance
Soul, this is your deliverance

The soul shall not repent
In fires that never relent
Where goes the soul?
Only they know
Where goes the soul?
Maybe onto woe

We may never know whilst living
The dead no hints are giving
We speak to them every day
When we visit where they lay

Graves do mark an empty ground
Here, the dead have no sound
You plead, pray and prove your
worth
Still, these souls are banned from
Earth

Where goes the soul?
The soul of a loved one
Where goes the soul?
Can they lurk beneath the sun?

THE IRRELEVANCE OF SIN
By Ish Baglisch

From the sky the stars are falling
No time to run, the Reaper's calling
Answer to the name of Charon
The Earth is now withered, barren

Swarms of death ride the wind
Careless to those whom have or
haven't sinned
They strip you down, a carcass worn
They leave your soul ripped and torn

Be all
End all
And all is ended
Ripped and torn
A soul can't be mended

End for
Die for
Upon a new beginning
Hell or Hades
Whom cares if you've been sinning

Weep the tears from sockets, empty
Burn they do in fires, tempting

Crying
Dying
Each and every day
Once again
Your soul they slay

Torture
Sought ya
In the deepest pit
Why run?
Torment is so quick

Weep the tears from sockets burning
For some peace this soul is yearning

THE KILL

By Ish Baglisch

I follow the
Unspoken command
Knowing I'm guided
By my master's hand

In seclusion
I wait
The target
Death create

Within my sights
I see him now
I'm the killer
On the prowl

I pull the trigger
He is dead
A life of corruption
He does shed

For lawlessness
I am paid
My master's pleased
A killer's been made

THE KILLING SPREE

By Ish Baglisch

Despite the fear I'm feeling
I refuse to take it kneeling
Despite the tightening noose
I fear the thunderous boom of Zeus

In deepest death I lay
Silent as the weeping eye
Though all about me voices scream
I know it's not a dream

The solemn stones whom poke from out
Upon the grass leaves blown about
Echoes in the waning light
Waiting, fearing coming night

Ghosts do gather on the ground
Wailing waul a wicked sound
With death about me I do see
Someone's been on a killing spree

Many dead are gathered here
Some too old to shed a tear
Still they moan ceaselessly
Of how Death took them cunningly

FIRE PATTERN

By Orran Cochrane

Patterns through the sky, glowing
Coalescing smoke growing
Despite the desperation felt before
Patterns pulse in Nevermore

Patterns on the picture, flowing
Into words the light is slowing
Enchanting us on patterned floor
Capture kills and static is sore

If you cannot find truth
Before the hangman's noose
If you cannot feel fire
More fuel will hasten her higher

If the pain will not relent
After death to fire sent
Burnt body on a pole
To Hell goes a wasted soul

Patterns in the fire, brightly
Flowing forward
Licking nicely
If you dare to enjoy
It will make you a Demon's toy

SEVERING OF HEART

By Pascle Ard

Come lay me down beside you
Tell me a lie that may come true
Open your heart to daily destruction
Build a bridge of heart's construction

How many times must that bridge
fall?
How loud should I call?
I need you and want you
Now I'm through

The bridge came down around my
ears
Heart is breaking
Save the tears
Tonight I dream
The dream will go on
Tonight ascend amongst the
throng....

....Of Angels you were born
My golden-haired love-torn
Loss of blood as runs from face
If this is death, I've packed my case

THE KNOWN TERROR

By Ish Baglisch

The terror you feel
In whole made real
The terror perceived
Shall never leave

Tremble and cower coward in fear
You always feel your death is near
At hand the doom you constantly elude
You fear damnation as what preludes

The heart of your terror
All you can endeavour
The fear of failure
To crosses nail ya

Endings are only beginnings
You fear you're soul is sinning
Death, a deliverance from your plight
Though still you fear eternal night

The terror you feel
In whole made real
The terror perceived
Shall never leave
From terror of grave
You can't be saved
From predominant doom
A deliverance soon

SHADOWS

By Jamess Johns

A shadow passes across my eyes
I am taken back there again
It is a dark and awful place
Where a soul can never mend

A shadow passes across my life
I will never be the same
I feel my soul is darker
Since this shadow came

I have a shadow in my heart
The darkest of them all
I wonder if this shadow portends
The downward spiral fall

I have a shadow in my soul
That, to Hell, will surely damn me
This shadow that does trail me
The Devil did surely hand me

FOOTSTEPS IN FIRE

By Edaff Pard

following footsteps into fire
Bound by all consuming wire
The plight left to me is dire

Wondering why the light has left
The darkness feels it will caress
Hearts are broken, bereft

In the dark the flame has risen
Revealing my unearthly prison
What the maker wants with me
Is beyond my comprehensibility

In the dark I have a vision
With one of the pieces missin'
I know not what to do
I do not know what ensues

Following footsteps out of fire
No longer bound by consuming wire
My plight is no longer dire

The light returns, it never left
Sun, he gives a slight caress
My heart no longer feels bereft

LAY

By Delroy Greene

Living is the price I pay
As I slowly rot away
Death is just a loser's game
In the end whom will I blame?
Empty, despite this life
Empty from toe to height
Flowing, the wounds have bled
Going, to the end I'm led

This must be the end of me
Blackness is all I see
This deliverance shall end in pain
In the end whom will I blame?

Empty, despite this life
Empty from toe to height
Flowing, the wounds have bled
Going, to the end I'm led

Forgotten, in death I lay
Rotting from day to day
Masking the pain once felt
Altars, before them knelt

Souls are sold every day
Eternal life beats slow decay
Sign the statement, it is done
Live in warmth beyond the sun

Down in Hell the fires tease you
With their screams the dead do tempt
you
Burn with them in Lucifer's lands
"Set all to flame," our master
commands

We ravage worlds and set them ablaze
Die the citizens in a smoking haze
Death is dealt in mortal realms
Dead Gods gutted leave spinning helms

LIFE FOREVER

By Delroy Greene

I have been a man broken by desire
I have stroked ice and patted fire
Like a stranger in the rain
I have found that Heaven is full of pain

The Devil has offered me a gift
Brought about an inner rift
Tore me apart, tempting sin
Now my tarot is very grim

The priest, he said, “the only way
Is to go to heaven and then there
stay”
I do not ever plan to die
That final breath I'll never sigh

The years have passed, I am still
alive
Not one family member, nor friend
survives
The years have taken them long ago
Now I watch the darkness grow

From far to near the darkness comes
Eating planets
Engulfing suns
In the hour of decision
Fate, a awful incision

Cut upon a jagged rock
Life forever in body locked
No pain can decide fate
No God can release you hate

PROMISES OF BELOW

By Joanne Axl

Promises of the shape below
In the dying fire
Feeding off the sinner
Fuelled by the liar
Promises of the pain below
Tortures of the Demon
Your meagre flesh
That holds your bones
Will more than likely feed 'em

Promises of the master below
Enter your deepest dreams
You pledge your life
To eternal strife
Damned you are, it seems

Promises of the life below
Make you want to cry
Morbidity dealt
Morose you've felt
Whose needs are fulfilled when you
die?

SLEEPING DEATH

By Prindle Rand

I promise you this
I don't lie
If you don't stay awake
I promise you'll die

Not to be melodramatic
Not to go overboard
If you sleep tonight
I'll banish you from the Lord
Death is an option
I'll offer you, friend
Death your deliverance
Death your end

Reapers arrive
All dressed in best
Standing before you
Upon a crest

They beckon, “come follow
We will release your sorrow”
They beckon with skeletal fingers
You follow, though your soul
cringes

LINGERING

By Keilor Cheswick

If the moon ever bled
From the sky, red
The lakes turned to blood
Red became the mud

The skies shone light
In deepest night
Eternity comes to an end
There, your soul he'll send

Forever death
Without breath
And there
Your soul left

Lingering death
Final breath
Earthly sigh
Left to die

OF DEATH
By Aaron Ungle

The sky wept blood
Until the land it flood
Death came down from the sky
No one knew why
Rivers turned red
The sky bled

Death came easy this day
Reaper bent low to take us away
As Heaven filled
Over spilled
Death drank more and more
We found ourselves at Hell's door

No invitation needed
Death surely succeeded
Me his child
In Hell piled
Skull on skull
Bone on bone
Death, sweet Death
Upon his throne

No invitation needed
The bell we heeded
Time for a killing
Heaven is spilling
We war with Angels
Their minions in white robes
Shall be slaughtered
If in the road
Of death

MASTER OF DEATH AND DISASTER

By Aaron Ungle

Raise my hate
Tempt my fate
If only I could find you again
Agony you will know by ten

Rest my case
Despise your face
Pain I will surely deliver
Just my gaze shall make you shiver

I am your answer
You are my cancer
Death will see you gone
To sharp my blade is hone

I am the master
Of death and disaster
I saw you to your grave
To Hell, no soul to save

One day I will die, too
That is a day you'll come to rue
The winged Demon
In fire beamin'
I torture this enemy
He is damned for eternity

MOVING DARKNESS

By Richard Feldar

Moving darkness
I realise
Nothing seen
But there are eyes
In this darkness
I've grown to hate
A sleepy dreaming
So sedate

Feeding and needing the darkness
Bleeding on my knees
Faces and places collide
Neither do appease

Moving darkness
I realize
Nothing seen
But there are eyes
Moving darkness
I abhor
I scream and scream
But all ignore

Fed and bled by darkness
Feed upon the light
Infernal shadow feeders
Work for blackest night

Taken to pieces delicately
You truly are delicious to me

MURKY WATERS

By Randle Westfolk

Sinking fast
With the weight of lead
Could it be
I am now dead?

Grasping for straws
None to be found
Will it be my epitaph
That I somehow drowned?

Murky waters
Closing over my head
Sinking faster
With the weight of lead

I come to rest
On a sandy bottom
It is destiny I stay
Until I am rotten

Fish taste flesh
This is death
Eternally rest
In murky waters

The waters claim
What is left
Hallowed ground
I've been bereft

Unsaid, the holy words
God cannot bless
No way out
Here, my body rests

Little fish I welcome thee
To partake in a feast
Body, brain bound by chains
All living ceased

MY GHOSTLY FRIEND

By Ann Daist

My ghostly friend, where are you
hiding?
Are you in the recesses, there
abiding?
Waiting for me in your lair
Deliver me an awful scare

My ghostly friend, what was your
name?
I remember you
You captured fame

It has been so long since you existed
To this day your soul has persisted
My ghostly friend, why wait you
here?
Invoking me to your fear
Better places you could be
Floating in Eternity's sea

My ghostly friend, why say
goodbye?
It is only the sun whom does rise
Coalescing quietly to a wisp
A fading soul my lips have kissed

MY MASTER'S SLAVE

By Jar Warrick

I find in dying embers
The answers which I sought
The fuel feeding the fire
Has a Hellish source

I gaze into the coals
I think of what to do
I can bring to the master
Souls whom scream anew

Within the fading fire
Encroaching, coming night
The wings of wicked wishes
Fly beyond my sight

Leaving dreams to dwell
Within these coalescing coals
I see those banished beyond
I welcome whispering souls

I see the simple silence
Screaming from my grave
In the black beyond
I become the master's slave

MY SECOND COMING

By Arid Arbrotten

Whom will have this soul once it
departs?
Whom will keep the centre?
Whom will keep the heart?

What roads will I walk?
Whom also treads this path?
When life unfetters, will another life
start?

This being affected by time
One day will play it's part
Will I freeze in Heaven?
Or burn on the Devil's hearth?

What answers will I bring
When I return to you?
Will my second coming
Mean life, for you, is through?

Do not look to me for answers
I hold no hidden truth
Why must all the cancers
Suck a soul in use?

BE NO MORE

By Estrel Olive

Delve the depth of your despair
Find a lightless hole in there
Enter all your empty rooms
Tolling is the bell of doom

At the very end of life you'll see
That of thee, very little there be
The lights will dim, one final time
Lifelessness the only sign

Be no more
Slam that door
In flood does pour your soul

In does pour your soul
To fill an empty hole

The dimming lights are now jet
black
Pathless tracks, no going back
Stay a while and you'll see
Nothing can become of thee

Be no more
Slam that door
In flood does pour your soul

In does pour your soul
To fill an empty hole

ALL ABOUT DEATH

By Terry Prowell

Viscous attack
Never come back
Out of the shadows
Hung at the gallows

Death has many forms
Not all are known
Sometimes it's quick
Other times you moan

Linger in Limbo
Burn in Hell
Float in the Abyss
Whom can tell?

Tickle the Devil
Make him laugh
Feed him blood
Sacrifice a calf

Be prepared with faithful service
Worship him upon Earth's surface
After death, after the show
It's good to have a friend where you
go

On Earth the faithful remain
Endangering life, many to be slain
We slit their throats, unforgiving
The Devil takes souls once living

KILLER

By Ish Baglisch

Death upon you
Death toward you
Death I have for you
Death is now on you

Face me forward
On the attack
I am killer
Killer's back

I am warrior
You know me
I am your death
To fight is glee

Bring me to my master early
Bring me to him later
Bring me to the one I serve
Send me to my maker

Satan, Lord, liege of all
I truly here thy call
I answered in a bath of blood
Pour to you my soul in flood

FREE FROM HELL

By Malcolm Fiddler

Nothing can last forever
All ties you must sever
Nothing is for sure
Our world is rotten to the core

Dying from within
Repenting all your sins
Nothing shall change
In Hell you shall remain

Certain words and certain symbols
Tempt you to your fate
The fires burn day and night
Be quick and don't be late

Of all the things taken from you
Your freedom you loved most
Now a pet for Devil's Demon
On fires you shall roast

BETTER YOU THAN ME

By Harriot Mare

You asked for it, Now you have it
A burning time for your crime
You wanted it, now you have it
A deathly cry when throat is dry
You needed it, now you got it
Heart in hand as was demanded

Now listen to the laughter
Blood and death, what comes after
Burning, burning, burning for
eternity
My friend, better you than me

You asked for it, now you have it
A burning time for your crime
You wanted it, now you have it
A deathly cry when throat is dry
You needed it, now you got it
Heart in hand as was demanded

BURIED

By Gypsy White

White light seeping throughout
A room so black and narrow
Clawing hands seek the light
With breathing slow and shallow

Scratching at the walls
Mouth a screaming maw
Hands are bloody tatters
Release is all that matters

Thumping from above
In that black and narrow room
Still my scream is silent
Now I face my doom

Buried alive
Can't survive
Without the light
None witness my plight

BURNING GAME

By Schipp Thane

Give the dead their space
In that place where they lay
The dead have a place
We hear what they say

Give the dead a name
To remember in the night time
Do the dead have fame?
We remember their life of crime

Crime and sin are both the same
Drive the dead completely insane
Purge the ghost
Where do they roast?
Is burning just a game?

Give the dead their peace
Why do we swear allegiance?
When dying makes you ceaselessly
Will you breathe in silence?

If the dead come for your soul
Will you fight the Demons?
In your little hole
The bugs and wyrmz do feed on

DECADE OF DECAY

By Angel Appenstock

He has come a final time
One of a long line
I must stay away
From the decade of decay

He has delivered a verdict
It is his precinct
It is the way I must stay
For a decade of decay

Eternally, an angry soul
Infernally I have been sold
Eternally, Demons play
Internally I decay

Readied for torture
Brain's closure
Being led away
From the decade of decay

Forever being for ever
A long time to wait
Eternity a day
In the decade of decay

Eternally, an angry soul
Infernally I have been sold
Eternally, Demons play
Internally I decay

BLACK ENOUGH

By Glen Glielg

Creep and crawl the creatures of the night
Dig a hole when comes the light
When blackness is down upon the land
Stars come out, as many as sand

The black, it eats
The black feasts
The black is alive
The black, it writhes

You think you're safe within God's
garden
Though when you feel your arteries
harden
You know the only solution for you
Is to die....and die you do

The black is back
The black has come
The black is he
The only one

Reaper, grim, he comes for you
Lead you to your judgment, true
Eternal presiders of wretchedness
Decide upon your wickedness

They send you down
They send you back
They send you into
Eternal black

Nothing lives in this dark hole
Nothing gives, the Devil stole
It crept upon silent feet
I swayed with it, like wind; the
wheat

Layer on layer of nothingness
Endless, unyielding this emptiness
Pray to your God, he won't listen
Your life you may be missin'

Wishing for some stimulation
Stars to form a simulation
Does the black wait for me
Black enough, this dreadful sea

Without a memory to which to hold
To Death your memories surely sold
Float you do in endless night
Beyond the dark, eternal plight

THE CARESSING DARK

By Elios Jones

So, they shone in our night
Now all gone
Away from sight

Despair greets all mankind
Loneliness seeks its own kind

Still, we linger in the sun
Despite his burning, tingling tongue

The poison enters all our pores
Creating weeping, cancerous sores

Death is release
It is a blessing
One day I shall cease
The dark is caressing

THE GOD'S IMMORTALITY
By Swit Reason

I enter into darkness
Following the wisp of a dream
Shedding all truth
I remember its strong beam

Everlasting sorrow
Dragon's breath
Touches of tomorrow
Unholy Death

Headless corpses litter the ground
To these souls you are bound
Breaking the boundaries of your
defeat
Still knowing tomorrow
Your future is bleak

Death, come swiftly from above
The last is dealt by hands of love
Know the endless bounds of reality
Now you have the God's immortality

BLISS OF DEATH

By Farra Kinkle

With one last breath
I surrender to Death
I wonder what will happen next

Black, but not encompassed
Tucked in, but not smothered
In this peace I reside
By myself abide

I am stripped
First of worry, then fear
Finally I lose my conscious thought
and just be

I am not lonely
I have no company
I conjure memories at will
So real the event reoccurs

Of God I have no doubt
Only he can create this bliss
The Devil exists
He is this bliss
This bliss is wickedness
If I had known death to be this
I would never had feared life

NAMELESS
By Virginia Vallens

A dying name cannot be saved
Fading, some words engraved
If you fear the failing night
By the moon a deadly quiet
A dying name cannot be said
Once, this tombstone could be read
Nothing moves, tears are craved
Fading words by ancients engraved

No one lives to serve the plot
Or mourn the body that does rot
No sons nor daughters nor daughter's sons
Come to bear the dying one

In this night all lovers mourn
Fading headstones are forlorn
Forever this terrible place does weep
All their souls, a Reaper keep

What is left without a name?
Whom comes to the corpse to place their blame?
Once the name has faded nothing is left
All hatred held is stagnant, bereft

TO SET FREE A SOUL

By Glen Glielg

Falling into a well of despair
Blackness prevails there
Loneliness, emptiness, sin and death
All left with your final breath

No longer shall I reach for light
Darkness I no longer fight
I greet my destiny with open arms
Praying to be sheltered from all the harms

He welcomes me with wide embrace
Mother of the deathskull face
He leads me into eternity
With a breath my soul is free

I wander worlds forgotten to time
I am but eternity's rhyme
A play on words for all to learn
Now I'm dead, for nothing yearn

Cease the dread
On darkness fed
Cease the worry and pain
Only peace remains

In dream I find
A peaceful mind
Pleasure beyond lifelessness
Given by father Death and his wife

HOMELESS SOUL
By Ann Daist

Death is but the beginnings
A journey to beyond
Through the gates of Hell I walked
Of fire I was fond

I have floated in the Ether
Into other worlds passed
Killed a mighty Dragon
I wear a leather mask

Through clouds to Heaven, entered
Saw an Angel, fair
Held her in my arms
Caressed her hair

Now, I wander Earth
Mountains, forests, swamps
I am a homeless soul
Whom goes where mind does
prompt

Upon a mountain I seat myself
I look over the land
To the right, mighty water
To the left, unending sand

I take to wing and fly above
This world I once did walk
I am the mountain air
On many winds I stalk

NEVERMORE

By Piese Woolworm

So bright the darkness that falls onto
me
The world is blackness as far as I can
see
No stars shall shine in this endless
night
All fade away
Away from sight

Spiraling into never, nowhere but
down
Falling more swiftly, nowhere bound

Swimming black oceans that never
have a shore
Wanting to breathe
I will nevermore

NIGHT FOREVER

By Anglish Dippea

Desperate in the dying hours to my
sins atone
No one near to hear repentance
My confessions, but a moan

Dreaming of Eternity in eternal light
For me there's nothing but blackness
An Abyss of eternal night
The stars have winked away
Out like buried sand
Night has come forever
Across my eyes, a hand

Crawling on my hands and knees,
seeking a holy place
Cringing from the black beyond, I
realize it has a face

The stars have winked away
Out like buried sand
Night has come forever
Across my eyes, a hand

RED WATER

By Dan Holmes

Wallowing in a drowning tub
Full of sharks whom draw my blood
Finding agony is all that's left
In this pain I am content

Reddest water does enfold
No redemption
No souls are sold
I seek a life other than this
Upon my head is placed a kiss

A spirit sentinel comes to assist
The parting of Death's hoary mist
Without the guidance or kiss of chance
I would wallow in deepest trance
Never would I dance

This life of mine which I take
Will welcome fires in which to bake
The blood-red water, so very cold
Death's arms are spread to enfold

The longest life to ever live
The holiest soul is but a sieve
There only for a soul's slaughter
Drowning in my reddest water

NO PATH IS CLEAR

By Aaron Ungle

I am damned beyond redemption
Never again will I see light of day
I am caught between completion
The scythe is ripe to slay

Finished, the end is near
Diminished, no path is clear

On this, the final hour
Of this, the dying flower
Raised to heights above belonging
Soon it is to come, the longing

Finished, the end is near
Diminished, no path is clear

On I go, above the clouds
Knowing woe beneath sun's shrouds
On I go above the garbage
Worlds of woe, to me, give homage

IN BLACK

By Joanne Axl

Black about I shout
Release me
Black enshrouds very loud
I can't see

Twisting in the Nether
No hope do I endeavor
No life to be reclaimed
In black not even pain

Hanging by thinnest threads
Fed upon unholy dread
It must be done
Do you agree?
From the black I cannot see

Is God hiding?
His time biding?
Release me
O, cloven hoof why aloof?
I can't see

I wish the black were burning
For some pain I'm yearning
I seek relief, if but brief
Anything but this blackened grief

Choking on the ash
Blinded by a flash
Why must I stay?
Does my body decay?
All is numb
Deaf and dumb
Release me
Is this fear?
I see so clear
I can see

Brightest light barred from sight
The moon and stars are black
Floating forever
No change in weather
Above me a tiny crack

Closer come, still deaf and dumb
I wonder what it be
I take a look
It is a hook
That digs deep into me

Shakes about
Makes me shout
A rag doll it has made
Rips apart
Tears the heart
To waste this soul's been laid

THE SOUL
By Dane Storm

A happy soul wandering
Through this cold domain
Never knowing fear
Never fearing pain
A lonely soul meandering
Through the stream of sky
Knowing no tomorrow
Forgetting it did die

The only soul considering
What the sun doesn't know
Through the clouds he blinks
Where'd our sun go

The flowing soul re-entering
The castle of the world
Around the light he's shimmering
Around the light he's curled

A glowing soul remembering
How it was to laugh
To hear the lively stories
Around a glowing hearth

A desperate soul failing
As memory is fading, too
Now this soul is returning
Returning now to you

IN BLACK YOU CHOKE

By Orran Ericson

You!
I see through you
Telling the things you do
Take what you command
This is what you planned
Underhand- so underhand

Peace
All living cease
Dealt with, doomed and damned
On and on I'm slammed-
Slammed-
Done all I can
Lead me to the light
Thrown into the night
Right
My plight is right
Stowing
My soul tonight

Is this where I stay?
Give me back the day
Nay!
You justly float
Damned, I'm telling you
Your soul just withdrew
What you knew, you knew
Infested the few with what you wrote
In black you choke

RELEASING REAPER

By Delroy Greene

Stones litter the ground
Bones, bitter, make no sound
Sacrifice the silent stonemaiden
Horded in a hoary haven

Winter finds the dead in graves
There's nothing there but souls to save
Winter has a fading face
They don't care in this dismal place

The trees do reach with dying fingers
Many souls are found whom linger
The trees hopelessly weep without sound
Upon the dead the rain does pound

A new one comes almost every day
Met the Reaper's mercy, scythe slay
A new one sheds the tears
Reaper released all pent up fears

THE SOUL IN DEATH ASSISTED

By Keilor Cheswick

Death the darkness draped over me
Blinded by blackness, I cannot see
Eternal night that doesn't have a feel
Before no altars do I kneel
Dragons awaken and deal me their pain
Death my deliverance, drive me insane

No pain
Not any more
No light
From behind any door
Just death
To deliver me from pain
Just Eternity
In which I must remain

Searching eyes are open to remorse
Nothing seen as Death through me
course
Sometimes I think I can run
Sometimes I remember the sun

Like the darkness I have no friends
Do all in this darkness end?
I have nothing
No heart to mend
I have nothing
No heart to rend

I wash my hands in eternal rivers
This, through mortal realms,
unknowingly slithers
I pass the light, it shines in my eyes
Reaching out as someone cries

Upon the verge I seat myself
To before, this is wealth
Seekers, whom number five
Searchers, whom I; survive
Visitor from another realm
Tortured takes the helm

Questions they have
All needing answers
Upon the board
A crystal dances

When they are done with me
They send me back to Eternity

Blinded
In darkness still
Sightless
My eyes are filled
Flowing
In nowhere creek
It was I
Whom Eternity seek

IN DEATH

By Crane Imbrose

How very high
Is the sky
Full of blue and white
How very loud
Is the cloud
Turning day to night

Evil comes
To me I s'pose
So slinking, dark and pure
I now await
My coming fate
The Reaper I have lured

Sweet taste of death
No more breath
Comes from this body, stilled
Guide me down
Below the ground
With maggots my eyes are filled

Here I stay
Without the day
In perpetual light
The priest was wrong
Death is a long
Rot without the light

Feasting frights
From the night
Descend upon my grave
They howl and tease
Do as they please
It is my fear they crave

A FINAL SELF-KILL
By Glen Glielg

Dreams the man of terrible things
Damnation's torture, broken
promises and sins
Name a price so it is paid
All the ghosts, to bed, been lain

Seek all things though finding
nothing
Means all beginnings, alpha bleeds
tragic
Lasting rattles in your chest
Rocking seed within the breast

Grant me
I need a place
Shan't see
Another caring face
Set free
To roam without will
Let it be
Another self-kill

SOULS IN THE SHADOWS

By Alse Olden

Among the shadows we do play
The descended darkness of a day
Within these recesses I abide
Where live all the creatures whom
have died

In these shadows I must stay
Until the darkness daytime slay
The night has never lied
With her I have sighed

I find the soul newly departed
Lead them to the fire, broken-hearted
Here from light they hide
Remembering tears cried

Within these shadows many souls
live
They swallow the dark which my
God gives
It is here that we decide
Within shadows abide

Souls in the shadows, each other
trust
Souls in the shadows erode like rust
Little remains but traces of time
Souls in the shadows know the
rhyme

Eternity's rhyme they have learnt
Hold no fear of being burnt
They know Hell's not worth pining
Souls in the shadows, always
rhyming

IN ROTTEN GRAVE

By Gypsy White

Dancing dead
Skull for head
By strings led
For master bled

Death came sweet
Lifeless meat
Tucked up neat
Within a sheet

Awakening scream
Sunlight's beam
Beyond a dream
Souls never redeem
The truth
Their youth
Their life
A lie it seems

Sweet light of day
Life I crave
I have death
In rotten grave

Gifted with a cloth
Haunted, my body rot
Left to meander meaninglessly
Left to rot eternally

A SOUL IN DARKNESS

By Verone Dorn

Slowly fading
With a greyer shading
Never seeing light again
Feeding darkness
That features starkness
Light was my only friend

Vortex whirling
And through it hurling
Will I ever see the end?
Tunnels closing
No light imposing
Where did God, my soul, send?

Into sorrow
I wish not to follow
I know now my soul shan't mend
Forever pining
On darkness dining
A lightless hole which has no end

THE SPIRIT CHOIR

By Agnus Adgit

Spirits gather around my hearth
Led along a lightless path
They moan as one stunningly
Of how Death took them cunningly

Now I tire of their game
If closely listen they'll drive me insane
I implore them, "go away"
But they stay

Now, in a circle they do sing
Around my head they form a ring
Deathly choir O, they bring
Woe to me, this gathering

Then they leave and I do wait
For Death to come, he won't be late
I gaze deep into the fire
Glad to be rid of spirit choir

THE DYING

By David Fistripper

The dying reach to realms unknown
Wishing to enter the world of bones
They writhe in torment
Not knowing a judgment
No longer do they float
Heaven is barred by a moat

Beyond the realm which holds no
hate
To a dying, fading race
I wait to recapture a flowing pulse
The Gods below are entirely false

If you ever want a light
That won't shatter in its own might
Perhaps your soul, to me, you'll sell
Then one day serve me in Hell

GRAVE SLEEP

By Aaron Ungle

The grave is but a place
To rest 'til you are bones
To reminisce the life
You once did own

Silent as a headstone
You lay in that lonely place
White cloth to keep you warm
A veil to hide your face

All is dark and brooding
Silence can be deep
No longer need you listen
Eyes are closed in sleep

You dream the many days
When life was full and whole
The days you wondered where
Lives the dearly departed soul

Laying in this peace
You wonder endlessly
Whom comes with flowers?
Whom comes for thee?

Are there naught but leaves
Blown about your grave?
Do you even care?
Is sleeping so depraved

The journey is not long
You arrived before you left
Leaving the world forlorn
Leaving loved ones bereft

SPIRITS

By Richard Feldar

The spirits are restless in the Ether
today
For they know it's there they must
stay
They are the air that tickles your face
Open your mouth, it's spirits you
taste

Paint my dreams in indigo
Through souls my dreams go
Never known I a soul to keep
For homeless souls do always weep

NOTHING LASTS

By Pascle Aird

Gone, without a trace
Gone, a forgotten face
Remains, nothing remains
Pain all slain

What is left but a heart, broken
In the night a love reawoken
Hovered above a sleeping form
A lost love now reborn

Conspiracies of silence
Sorceries so violent
What to do with that which slays
Passes all the lazy days

So what to do in shadows?
Nothing matters much
So what to do with shadows?
Shadows cannot touch

Leaving life completely
Forgotten in the past
Death enfolds completely
Nothing's made to last

COMFORTS OF DEATH

By Alton Edwards

Under the moonlight
In a shadowy grave
I lay awake but death I crave

My friend the moon
Through branches shine
Casting shadows where crawlers
dine

Less I have
More I need
My skin is torn but I don't bleed

A longing for life
A thirst for death
The Reaper came and left I guess

I seek an eternal rest
A heart once beat in this chest
The Reaper came and left I guess
Refusing me the comforts of death

GRAVEYARD

By Ellis Wile

Wilting flowers on a grave
Signifies a soul's been saved
Never strays from hallowed ground
In this place, betrayal, a sound

Plastic flowers blown about
Morose the wind which blows
throughout
Leafless trees prove a curse
Set within this ground to nurse

Stony sentinels guard the ghosts
Vacant are the holy hosts
Only death permeates this population
Sacred is this slow cremation

Upon a hill a stranger stands
He is reaching out with empty hands
Never had he seen a land
So full but yet so empty
This is his cemetery

He clears the weeds
Plants some seeds
With duty done
He'll have some fun

In the house of hallowed dead
He imagines blood being shed
He mounts a corpse, innocent,
inanimate
Penetration becomes imminent

Not a sound this corpse makes
As the keeper death's cherry takes
When deed is done her soul is
damned
When seed has cum Death takes her
hand

He says farewell, a bid goodbye
To the corpse before him lay
Desecrated she does blush
Pale skin expertly brushed

He likes his corpses blue
When death he sees anew
He takes them
Paints them
Thanks them for the screw

All dressed up in Sunday's best
Readied for eternal rest
One last time they say goodbye
Children, parents and friends all cry

SWEET REVENGE

By Lerric Moyal

Dreams bleed from my eyes
Red weeps from the skies
The clouds have turned to black
At the end I know I'm not coming
back

Death is just an existence
A state other than we know
We leave our empty bodies
We don't really go

Illusion fades away
On this bloody day
The skies have turned to red
The color of blood I bled

I find the one whom killed me
I swoop low to haunt
I drive him completely mad
With bloody promises and Hellish
taunts

Sweet revenge is mine
On his fear I dine
I watch his suicide
Another killer died

Damned to float the Nether
Among the storm, a feather
Blown about remorselessly
Made to feel pain endlessly

O, SWEET DEATH

By Lerric Moyal

O, sweet death
How swift you come
First ignored
But now the one

Reaper comes, deathcap sweet
Carve my soul, lifeless meat
Take a heart and squeeze a hand
No longer can I stand

Skeletal grip on scythe, sharp
Bring it down upon my heart
I wonder if I'll hear the harp
Once among the dead

It's blackness that I seek
The endless flow of Nowhere creek
Where, for Eternity I spend my strife
An abysmal hole of empty life

WRITHE NOT RUST

By Ellis Wile

Death warms within most minds
A hollow existence all he finds
With licking, lurking lust he sees
A soul to unlock the body's keys

When the soul is free to wander
When the soul is his to plunder
Beware the light which insists
Beware the night where evil exists

The body, empty without a soul
Fused together they make a whole
When Death comes with scythe to
reap
The soul and body will never be
complete

One is left for writhing wyrmz
Again alive in agony squirms
The other enters eternal night
Or descends into a dire plight

All I know
All I trust
When alive I cannot rust
If iron I were and rain did come
I would worry in God's harsh sun

ALL THE ILL

By Roo Philp

I promise to return from fiery sea
Tell you all that happened to me
The whole truth and not a lie
I will tell you what happens when we die

The promise of pain death does inflict
Will make you, my friend, very sick
If you think a trumpet calls
Just remember, Lucifer falls

I will tell you of judgment, harsh and
true
I will speak of fire which sears
through
I will inform you of Demons whom
love to fulfill
The things I speak of
All the ill

I hear you whine, plead and pray
One last thing I have to say
"I doubt there is a Heaven
For Hell you should be preparin'
Of God I know naught
The Devil my soul bought"

TIME IN ETERNITY

By Lillia Love

What do you call the blackness?
A feast it makes of your brain
What thrives in darkness?
Does evil have a name?

When clouds in sky are streaked
with grey
Shadowed is the Earth
On your knees you stop and pray
Or lose all sense of worth

The God's almighty fury
Comes to you in grave
A voice of suppressed wrath
Says you have no soul to save

RUN, HIDE AND FLEE

By Aceed Akmed

Names of doom upon the lips
Reality folds, then open rips
Pouring through the hole
Come the blackened souls
They are here for a killing
Sightless eyes are chilling

Run, you cannot hide
Run, they all lied
Flee for your life
Flee from the strife

They track you down by beat of heart
They rip the flesh on bones apart
Dead now, you face the woe
Because every day this is all you know

Run, you cannot hide
Run, they all lied
Flee for your life
Flee from the strife

ERUPTIONS OF VIOLENCE

By Leo Cloud

When anger is silent
It erupts in violence
Though dying does have a call
When heard by millions
I know what a kill brings
And where plummeting souls fall

The coming decadence
The hate-filled death dance
After what was God's own fall
The merry murderer
The sinful sturdier
What was heard by one affected all

The screaming tyrant
Erupts in violence
This hatred found in us all
Without this pattern
The four rings of Saturn
Will bring to the Earth a silent squall

ANGUISH

By Vee Shaeffer

Anguish in her purest form
On wind shall be reborn
From Heaven blow
To down below
Leaving me forlorn

Anguish in its simplest state
Comes from depth, the Devil create
Sweep through me
Blind, can't see
Leave me to the fates

Anguish is her unknown name
Is never caught, cannot be tamed
It takes you
It makes you
Distinguishes love from pain

Anguish sews within the breast
A seed which causes me unrest
Comes undone
Sewn in some
The final, futile test

TO DIE

By Richard Feldar

Despair crawls through my heart
Melancholy never departs
Morose, the way I hang my head
Spilling tears made blood red

Worsening with the waning day
Blackened souls crave to stay
Never leaving
Always seething
Prayers given, night receding

Day brings no release
Will this heart cease?
Fade with the fallen face
The beating heart still keeping pace

Releases and realizes it's mistakes
Pump the blood for no one's sake
Decide to sever the cord
Be sent back to the Lord

Many people come and mourn
Above you breathless corpse
Some cry, some kiss, other's you
miss
This parting is enforced

If this day you decide to leave
To visit God in Heaven
Know that one day you will return
You'll visit me quite often

ETERNAL SOUL
By Mirrabai Das

Once, upon a midnight breeze
Feeling slowly my soul ease
I cast about for sainted ones
They've withdrawn as sets the sun

A child's heart in all the spirits
On winds they cry, listen; hear it
The darkness now engulfs the sound
All these souls go underground

A final prayer from dog to moon
An eerie, tempting, Siren's tune
How many days have passed like
this
Until the sun, the hills, does kiss

Mighty dawn rules the land
Earth now under his command
Many days and nights have passed
Many more will before the last

Eternal souls are free to wander
They loiter and lovingly ponder
They don't heed another being
The light of the sun they're seeing

ANSWERS FROM A HEADSTONE

By Delroy Greene

I stand within the graveyard beside
the trees and tombs
Because it is now early spring the
trees are out in bloom
I kneel beside the headstone of one
lost long ago
With no tears within these eyes I
wonder where they go

No answers come and the wind picks
up a bit
No answers come and I stand from
where I sit
I turn my back on them, the stone,
the box, the bones
I turn my back on them and face my
death alone

FEAR THE GRAVE

By Stone Dull

Swimming in a lake of fire
Beyond all hope there is desire
Drowning in the endless black
A Godly past your soul does lack

With every death the Devil lets go
All these souls are led to woe
The Reaper, Grim does answer all
A final breath is Reaper's call

Long ago there was a light
Shining bright in infinite night
Then it shattered to tiny stars
Shine did they, the column's shards

As our sun bids goodbye
All do hear his earthly sigh
We make believe we're bold and
brave
All in dark do fear the grave

If Reaper comes to you in sleep
If he has a scythe to reap
Your soul belongs to the light
He comes for you in the night

Tremors tremble down your spine
Upon your fear the Reaper dines
He has you now in skeletal hand
'Follow me', is his command
Above the world, hover we
Beautiful as the Earth's sea
In this gift I know as death
Corporeal lungs have no breath

Souls do beat with pulsing light
Many colors shining bright
A coalition of many sounds
Through Heaven melodically pounds

As all the souls gather near
The song of souls engulf our fear
They promise Death will release
Bring about a soul's peace

AWAY FROM THE LIGHT

By Ellis Wile

Dead on deliverance
Never breathe again
For your beligerance
And ignorance, my friend

Come to the answer
You never thought to be
Watch the dancer
Twist incredibly

First rays of dawn break the dark
Now open on a fist of pain
Death the deliverance given
In death you must remain

Answers come beyond you
Beyond your comprehension
In a dismal place
Feeling forgotten tension
Dance all you like
Away from the light
Dance away from the light

Harmful rays inflict such pain
Away from the light I wish to remain
The blood I have spilt
The souls I have stole
Suck me into a shining hole

Beyond the hole, I know, is fate
Judgment day, I won't be late

THE FINAL FALL

By Angus Ungle

Feed the bugs
Feed the grubs
Slithering slugs of Beelzebub's

Worship wyrm
Dirt milkshake
Slide and squirm
Human steak

Loosing juice
Eyeballs loose
Shedding skin
Silent din

Degrade
Nothing you will be
Strayed
Never to be free
Invade
The carrion come to call
Remade
Before the final fall

THE FINAL SAY (OF WHERE YOU LAY)

By Leo Cloud

Like rats around a day old corpse
Like specters in the mist
We are born to come and go
The Reaper does insist

Be fire releasing sorrow
Or in the earth for all tomorrow
Be it waves recapture
Or rapped in rags of rapture

Let the darkness in
It is a wondrous thing
Let the Devil take you
Eternal fire take you

Have the final say
Of where your body lay
Cleansed in the fire
Cleansed in the pit

Beyond tomorrow
Beyond today
No more sorrow
Where do you lay?

NOTHING TO GIVE

By Rowan Ward

Never read the end of a book first
Never speak the name of the one
you've cursed
Bleed all you wish but never spill it
Keep close the memory but never
kill it

Be good but die young
Be yourself but never have fun
Chase that cloud, never to catch it
Burn your house but do not play with
matches

Die in life
Soul's strife
Dying to live
Nothing to give

Finish the game whenever a winner
Have your last meal
Have your last dinner
Die and be dead, never to have lived
Forgotten already, what did you
give?
A prisoner of a padded cell
With only four walls to hear you yell
Yell the story of your shattered
existence
Your heart pounds only with
persistence

Die in life
Soul's strife
Dying to live
Nothing to give

www.ingramcontent.com/pod-product-compliance
Ingram Content Group UK Ltd.
Pitfield, Milton Keynes, MK11 3LW, UK
UKHW020241250726
13967UKWH00001B/492

9 781470 915155